CONTENTS

About Paz & Associates
and *Reading Group Choices*

One of the goals of Paz & Associates is to join with publishers, bookstores and libraries to develop resources and skills that promote books and reading.

Reading Group Choices is distributed annually to bookstores, libraries, and directly to book groups. Titles from previous issues are posted on our website at **www.readinggroupchoices.com**. Books presented here have been recommended by book group members, librarians, booksellers, literary agents, publicists, authors, and publishers. All submissions are then reviewed to ensure the "discussibility" of each title. Once a title is approved for inclusion, publishers are then asked to underwrite production costs, so that copies of *Reading Group Choices* can be distributed for a minimal charge.

For additional copies, please call your local library or bookstore, or you may contact us by phone or email as shown below. Quantities are limited. For more information, please visit our websites at **www.pazbookbiz.com** and **www.readinggroupchoices.com**

800/260-8605 — mkaufman@pazbookbiz.com

INTRODUCTION

If it's true that "Imitation is the most sincere form of flattery," those of us in book groups should have swelled heads by now. A quick look at this year's collection of titles finds no less than three different books—both fiction and nonfiction—for and about reading groups.

Take *Angry Housewives Eating Bon Bons*, by Lorna Landvik, for example. Or *The Blackberry Tea Club* by Barbara Herrick. We've even introduced a bestselling British novel by Elizabeth Noble titled, aptly enough, *The Reading Group*.

Is it really that much of a stretch to think that people could form such strong bonds, have such meaningful conversations, and form friendships that last for years? Hardly! From what we hear, reading groups, more than ever before, are attracting both men and women, mothers and daughters, teenagers—readers and book-lovers of every size, shape, color and temperament—to broaden their horizons and enrich their lives.

Perhaps one of the appeals of book groups is the ability to connect with like-minded people, especially when such connections might not exist in our own family units or in an increasingly fragmented society. What goes on in families is another dominant theme in this year's collection of titles: close family ties, dysfunctional communication, pain and suffering, loss, exuberant joy, secrets buried and revealed. Our own family lives are made more complete by identifying—or not—with these touching and intimate portraits. As Pat Conroy said of *The Turtle Warrior*, one of our featured titles, "...[It's] a family you'd never want to be a part of, but it is one you will never forget."

You'll also find some thought-provoking and soul-searching books that will lead you to feeling more whole, and more positive about the possibilities for our communities and the world around us.

In today's "hyper" culture—more and faster—there's nothing like the written word, especially in the form of a good book, to regain a fresh perspective. Whether for your book group's discussion or your own personal enjoyment, we hope that you'll enjoy this year's collection of "discussible" books.

Mark Kaufman   Donna Paz Kaufman

THIS YEAR'S FEATURED TITLES

ALL THAT MATTERS

Author: Jan Goldstein

Publisher: Hyperion, 2004

Website: www.hyperionbooks.com

Available in:
Hardcover, 208 pages. $17.95
(ISBN 1-4013-0110-X)

Subject: Family Life/
Personal Discovery (Fiction)

Summary

Twenty-three year old Jennifer Stempler has nothing left to lose: the love of her life dumped her, her mother died in a senseless car accident, and her famous Hollywood producer father started a brand-new family—with no room in it for her. So Jennifer decides to pursue peaceful oblivion in an attempt on her own life. But Jennifer's depression is no match for her Nana's determination. Gabby Zuckerman refuses to let her granddaughter self-destruct and whisks Jennifer back to her home in New York City, intending to prove to Jennifer that her life cannot possibly be over yet. In fact, it has just begun. Gabby teaches Jennifer how to trust and hope again. And by relating her own tragic and heroic experience during the Nazi occupation of Poland, Gabby bestows upon Jennifer an understanding of life's value.

Recommended by: Faye Kellerman

"An uplifting story of the generations, exploring that special bond between grandchild and grandparent."

Author Biography

Jan Goldstein is an award-winning poet and playwright and the author of two works of nonfiction: **Life Can Be This Good** and **Sacred Wounds: Succeeding Because of Life's Pain**. An ordained rabbi, he lives with his wife and children in Los Angeles.

Topics to Consider

1) Why does Jennifer feel life is not worth living? By attempting suicide, what is she trying to prove, and to whom is she trying to prove it? What does she mean when she says, "Suicide is not an act of confusion, but of clarity?" Discuss what you might say to Jennifer about this statement, and why.

2) Describe Gabby. Why is Gabby the "last person" Jennifer wants to see when she wakes up in the hospital?

3) When Gabby says, "Jennifer is missing everything that really matters," what does she mean? What are some of the reasons or excuses that Jennifer might offer if she could acknowledge why she is missing what matters?

4) Consider Gabby's question, "What kind of God takes a young mother and leaves an aging, unhealthy Grandmother?" Why do you think these things happen? How do they test one's spiritual and moral beliefs?

5) How is Gabby's struggle during the Holocaust similar to Jennifer's struggle? What does Gabby share with her granddaughter that changes Jennifer's life?

6) How does Gabby use the "letting go" ceremony on the rock in Maine to relinquish her self-guilt? Are there rituals or acts you've witnessed that inspired you to action? How does letting go of her self-guilt allow Jennifer to make different choices about her life, to move on?

7) If you are involved with people older or younger than yourself, share what each generation can give to the other.

8) Consider sharing the "gifts of the day" with those in your life. Is this something you do regularly? What are some of the "gifts" that you might share today if asked? Why is this important?

9) What is the significance of the title, *All That Matters*? What does it mean to you? What does author Jan Goldstein believe about "all that matters"? Discuss what matters most to you.

For a complete reader's guide, visit www.hyperionbooks.com

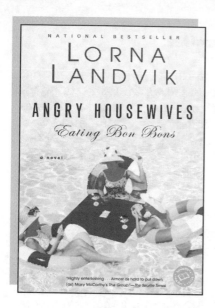

ANGRY HOUSEWIVES EATING BON BONS

Author: Lorna Landvik

Publisher: Ballantine, 2003

Website:
www.ballantinereaderscircle.com

Available in:
Paperback, 432 pages. $13.95
(ISBN 0-345-44282-2)
Mass market paperback, $7.99
(ISBN 0-345-47569-0)

Subject: Women's Lives/
Friendship (Fiction)

Summary

The women of Freesia Court are convinced that there is nothing good coffee, delectable desserts, and a strong shoulder can't fix. Laughter is the glue that holds them together—the foundation of a book group they call AHEB (Angry Housewives Eating Bon Bons), an unofficial "club" that becomes much more. It becomes a lifeline. Holding on through forty eventful years, this stalwart group of friends depicts a special slice of American life, of stay-at-home days and new careers, of children and grandchildren, of bold beginnings and second chances, in which the power of forgiveness, understanding, and the perfectly timed giggle fit is the CPR that mends broken hearts and shattered dreams.

Recommended by: *The Denver Post*

"It is impossible not to get caught up in the lives of the book group members....Landvik's gift lies in bringing these familiar women to life with insight and humor."

Author Biography

Lorna Landvik is the bestselling author of *Patty Jane's House of Curl*, *Your Oasis on Flame Lake*, *The Tall Pine Polka*, and *Welcome to the Great Mysterious*. She is also an actor, playwright, and proud hockey mom. Her latest novel is coming out in May 2005.

Topics to Consider

1) During the sixties and seventies, the Angry Housewives smoked cigarettes and threw back highballs—even while pregnant—without knowledge of the harm it could do. If they could have glimpsed their futures then, what do you think would have surprised them most about their future selves? What is one thing you know now that you would have really appreciated being aware of ten years ago?

2) Why do you think groups like AHEB—women who live near each other, raise children together, and bond over books together—persist even in a climate of working moms and in a culture that is flooded with other types of media?

3) Discuss Faith's letters to her deceased mother. What kind of catharsis do they provide Faith, and how do the tone and nature of the letters change as the years go by?

4) Audrey gets a kick out of introducing Kari to strangers as a recently released convict. Discuss the women's jokes, nicknames, and embarrassing moments—how does humor work to solidify friendship?

5) Kari faces a critical decision when Mary Jo forbids her from telling Anders that the baby is his grandchild. Would you be able to keep such a secret? For which character is this secret most constructive; for which is it most destructive?

6) How do you feel about the later inclusion of Grant as a member of AHEB? Did you think the inclusion of a male affected their particular group dynamic? What is valuable about inviting men to participate in women's dialogue?

7) Merit eventually finds Paradise, literally and figuratively. Do you believe that good things come to people who wait?

8) This book covers a lot of ground, both personal and political. What do you think is the most important lesson these women learn over thirty years? Which characters were most ripe for change with the political and cultural tide? Whose story did you think most embodied the emergence of women as a growing force outside the home?

For additional topics, visit www.ballantinereaderscircle.com

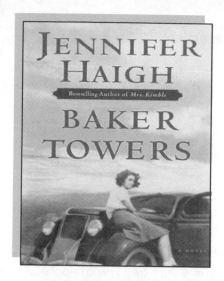

BAKER TOWERS

Author: Jennifer Haigh

Publisher: Wm. Morrow (Jan. '05)

Website: www.jenniferhaigh.com

Available in:
Hardcover, 352 pages. $24.95
(ISBN 0-06-050941-4)

Subject: Family Life/
Americana (Fiction)

Summary

In the coalmines of western Pennsylvania, Stanley Novak endured backbreaking work alongside scores of men just like him, immigrants or the sons of immigrants providing for their families in close-knit Bakerton, a town named for its mine. Bakerton is home to all five of Stanley's children, though he will not live to see them reach adulthood. His widow, Rose, will watch their oldest son, George, become a soldier in World War II. Their daughter Joyce will join the military as well, hoping the Air Force can give her opportunities that working-class Bakerton could not. Their daughter Dorothy will take a job in Washington, D.C., where her fragile beauty and romantic ideals make her dangerously vulnerable. Their two youngest children will struggle to fill the empty emotions of growing up without a father while seeking a world far beyond his. But at each turning point in love or fortune or work, the siblings can't forget the beacon of home.

Recommended by: *Fort Worth Star-Telegram*

*"The question is not whether Haigh might turn out to be a good writer. Rather, we have the intriguing possibility that **the next great American author is already in print.**"*

Author Biography

Jennifer Haigh is the author *Mrs. Kimble*, which won the PEN/Hemingway Award for first fiction. Her short stories have appeared in *Good Housekeeping*, the *Hartford Courant, Virginia Quarterly Review*, and elsewhere. She lives in Hull, Massachusetts.

Topics to Consider

1) Do the opening paragraphs depict Bakerton as an oppressive community or a utopia, or a combination of the two? Viewing the town itself as a character, how would you describe its biography?

2) Discuss the social distinctions embodied in the Novak family. What roles did society prescribe for Rose and Stanley, based on gender and class? Did their children lead more fulfilling lives than their parents?

3) Do you attribute the differences between the siblings to temperament or circumstance? How was each one affected by Stanley's death?

4) Before meeting Rose, Antonio Bernardi had never seen an Italian wife on Polish Hill. In what ways has the American immigrant experience, and the character of immigrant communities, changed over the past century?

5) Joyce's intellectual drive is accompanied by a strong dose of practicality. Do you view her as the family's savior or as a wet blanket? Why do so many of her efforts go unappreciated?

6) What does Lucy convey about the nature of hunger, and the nature of beauty? What is the significance of her eventual role as healer?

From an Interview with Jennifer Haigh

Q. Was *Baker Towers* inspired by your own family history?

A. Yes and no. The characters themselves are inventions; they don't resemble anybody in my family. But the details about the town itself, what life was like in the postwar years, definitely came from my parents and other relatives. *Baker Towers* ends in the Vietnam era, right around the time I was born, so I couldn't rely on my own memories of the period I was writing about. By the time I came along, the coal mines were already in decline. The era of the company town was past, and the region was on its way to become something else. But I grew up hearing about how things used to be, and when I set out to write this book I had a wonderful time interviewing family members about what life was like when coal was king.

For more Discussion Topics and a full Author Interview,
visit www.jenniferhaigh.com

THE BLACKBERRY TEA CLUB
Women in Their Glory Years

Author: Barbara Herrick

Publisher: Conari Press, 2004

Website: www.redwheelweiser.com

Available in:
Paperback, 176 pages. $12.95
(ISBN 1-57324-965-3)

Subject: Women's Lives/
Personal Discovery (Nonfiction)

Summary

Mid-life crisis is not a crisis—it is a passage into joy. This was the essential truth discovered by the four women of a certain age, founding members of the Blackberry Tea Club, which began as late-night conversations while sipping blackberry tea with a little kick added. Those conversations about children, men, jobs, weight, clothes, food, travel, gossip, politics, medicine, healing, spirituality, adventure, and books grew slowly, beautifully into the Blackberry Tea Club. They discover the Glory Years for women, years that bring about the expansion and reorganizing of the mind, heart, and spirit, and the birthing of a larger self of immense compassion, intellect, will, spirit, love, and capability.

Recommended by: *Publishers Weekly*

"... Simple and straightforward, it will resonate with women who prefer to see the inevitable emotional upheaval that accompanies aging as 'a spiritual passage' rather than a midlife crisis."

Author Biography

Barbara Herrick is a writer whose work includes two books about Boise, Idaho, as well as numerous poems and stories. She is a founding member of the Blackberry Tea Club.

Topics to Consider

1) Most women are entering their midyears on a healthy, positive note. Why are we portrayed as unhealthy, whiney, spendy, self-absorbed, obsessed with the loss of our looks, and, sometimes, decidedly odd, if not a little nuts in our culture and media?

2) The urgency of health, for wholeness, for meaning, for adventure becomes acute during our 40s and 50s. What "awakenings" have moved you into a better place?

3) Our stories of menopause are so personal and profound. They shape our perceptions of our lives for the next three decades. What is your story? What helped you? What drove you right over the brink? What were its great gifts?

4) If there is a thing that keeps us young, it is the ability to learn. We are tackling the arts, movement, languages, and technology, all of it. What keeps you buzzed up now? What would you like to learn? What sends you into the depths of life? Or engaged with the beginner's mind?

5) Our love is enlarging, engaging us, moment to moment, in the movement and shape of the world. What are the stories of "Big Love" that guide you, which opened your soul to love's magnanimity, that made it possible for you not only to "live large," but also to "love large?"

6) This book is generous and embracing of men. What great good have men brought into your life? Make a gratitude list. Show them your list. Ask them to read the book. They have a right to their own Glory Years.

7) Our Glory Years are the years we reshape the dreams we left behind as we grew responsible, parental, spousal, or employable. What new/old dreams would give your life meaning, texture, and worth? What are three steps you can take (without destroying your family or financial life) in the next year that would bring those dreams to fruition? What would make your Glory Years healthy and happy?

BROKEN FOR YOU

Author: Stephanie Kallos

Publisher: Grove Press, 2004

Website: www.groveatlantic.com

Available in:
Hardcover, 384 pages. $24.00
(ISBN 0-8021-1779-1)

Subject: Women's Lives/
Friendship (Fiction)

Summary

The worlds of two women in self-imposed exile are transformed when their paths intersect. Margaret Hughes is a septuagenarian, who lives alone in a mansion in Seattle with only a massive collection of valuable antiques for company. Enter Wanda Schultz, a young woman with a broken heart who has come to Seattle to search for her wayward boyfriend. When Margaret opens her house to the younger woman, everything begins to change. As their friendship evolves, secret pasts are revealed and reclaimed, launching a series of remarkable and unanticipated events.

Recommended by: Sheri Holman, author, *The Dress Lodger*

"...A story of broken hearts and broken promises, it is also the story of the ways we put things back together...Kallos is a novelist to watch, and one who, mercifully, still believes in happy endings."

Author Biography

Stephanie Kallos spent twenty years in the theater as an actress and teacher, and her short fiction has been nominated for both a Raymond Carver Prize and a Pushcart Prize. She lives in Seattle with her husband and two children. *Broken for You* is her first novel.

Topics to Consider

1) An unlikely heroine, Margaret is an old, peculiar recluse. How is her diagnosis an inciting force for change? Talk about her growing appreciation of the uncommonness of common things.

2) Margaret and Wanda, as close as they are, each retain core secrets until almost the end. Why? And what are the secrets? Why does M. J. Striker withhold his own secret and recognition so long? How much is it really possible to know another person?

3) Did you find conflicts between traditional values and newer ones? Where? Which characters grow larger or more sympathetic from being challenged by younger people? Does the converse hold?

4) What does it mean to bear witness in this book, and why does it matter? For instance, why does it matter to honor the dead and find out their stories and try to fulfill their wishes?

5) How does the fact that neither Margaret nor Wanda is Jewish affect their joint efforts vis-à-vis the Holocaust victims and memories? When does expiation for her Nazi-sympathizer father become important for Margaret?

6) Discuss Stephanie Kallos's definition of a relationship [p. 295]. Do you find her view of human behavior to be alarming? Or do you find it oddly comforting?

7) How is the poetry of Yeats interwoven in the book? Why in particular should it be Yeats who recurs?

8) How are love and sex recurring symbols of healing and joy? Think about specific relationships, those that survive and those that don't. Describe M.J.'s loves, both as Striker and as O'Casey. How do you compare young love to that of older people? Why does Wanda wait so long to accept Troy as her lover? What does the parenthood of Susan and Bruce say about love, sex, and family?

For a complete reader's guide, visit www.groveatlantic.com

THE CENTER OF EVERYTHING

Author: Laura Moriarty

Publisher: Hyperion, 2004

Website: www.hyperionbooks.com

Available in:
Paperback, 335 pages. $14.00
(ISBN 0-7868-8845-8)
Hardcover, 304 pages. $22.95
(ISBN 1-4013-0031-6)

Subject: Family Life/
Personal Discovery (Fiction)

Summary

Ten-year-old Evelyn Bucknow tries to make sense of an unruly world spinning around her. Growing up with a single mother who is chronically out of work and dating a married man, Evelyn—very often expected to play the role of the adult—learns early how to fend for herself. Readers will find a searing rendering of the claustrophobia of small town midwestern life, as seen through the eyes of a teenage girl. Evelyn must come to terms with the heartbreaking lesson of first love—that not all loves are meant to be—and determine who she is and who she wants to be. Stuck in the middle of Kansas, between best friends, and in the midst of her mother's love, Evelyn finds herself...in *The Center of Everything*.

Recommended by: Anna Quindlen, *Book-of-the-Month Club News*

"Authentic and intelligent ... One of those novels that makes you feel sad when it's over."

Author Biography

Since earning her M.A. from the University of Kansas, **Laura Moriarty** won the George Bennett Fellowship for Creative Writing at Phillips Exeter Academy. This is her first novel. She's at work on her next novel and lives in Lawrence, Kansas.

Topics to Consider

1) What do you think of Evelyn, Tina, and Eileen? What about Tina's father? What kind of people are they? What do they look like? What is Sam's role in the family and in the story? Share your impressions of other characters that stand out, and why.

2) Examine and discuss whether or not Evelyn's thoughts and spoken words are reflective of a child's point of view, and why. Share some examples that you find effective and/or moving.

3) How do Evelyn's feelings about her mother affect your feelings about Tina? Explore whether or not you are sympathetic or disgusted by Tina, and why. Share some examples of how Moriarty brings out the mother/daughter relationship and whether or not you can relate to it, and why.

4) What are the roles of friendship pins and particular pieces of clothing in the lives of grade-school kids? What are your memories and experiences of these years? Share whether or not you think Moriarty successfully conveys these school experiences, and why.

5) Discuss the use of religion as a recurring theme throughout the book. As a storytelling device, what purpose does it serve? Why would a man as "religious" as Tina's father shun his daughter and be so unforgiving? How does Eileen live her beliefs? How does religion affect Evelyn?

6) Why does Moriarty use the struggle between evolution and creationism in the story? Examine whether or not the characters' positions ring true, and why. What would you say to those who have different beliefs than yours?

7) How does the car accident that kills Traci affect Evelyn? What motivates Evelyn to initially keep Traci's belongings hidden?

8) Discuss the underlying theme throughout the novel of being chosen or not being chosen.

For a complete reader's guide, visit www.hyperionbooks.com

EMOTIONAL DECEPTION

Author: David Robinson

Publisher: Platinum One, 2004

Website:
www.PlatinumOnePublishing.com

Available in:
Paperback, 228 pages. $13.95
(ISBN 0-9752702-0-6)

Subject: Relationships/
Social Issues (Fiction)

Summary

Emotional Deception takes readers on a journey of distressing drama, and describes how clashing differences can destroy a family in America. It's a suspenseful story, revolving around Dr. Epstein, who makes a desperate and eventually failed attempt to control his wife, Jennifer...all the while not realizing that Jennifer's fate was already sealed by her own murky past. Suddenly and unexpectedly, his insecurities erupt as he changes face and starts reacting out of emotions. As reality kicks in, both come to the realization that compromise and change are now buried in their past—and their lifetime commitment was shadowed with dishonesty and deceit. As more and more of their respective skeletons surface, all hell breaks loose.

Recommended by: Patricia Woodley, Dialogue Book Club

"It's one of the most discussed book topics in my social circle today— Relationship Drama. If you can read just one book this year, **Emotional Deception** *is the book to read."*

Author Biography

David Robinson holds degrees in Journalism and Marketing Management, and has written numerous articles in publications regarding change management in technology and social issues reflecting today's societal ills. He resides in Chicago, Illinois, where he is currently an Adjunct Instructor at Chicago State University.

Topics to Consider

1) Is it possible for someone to harvest "skeletons in the closet" from the person whom they have been married to for more than ten years? Should Jennifer have forgiven Daniel for harboring such a secret?

2) What is the dynamic between Dr. Epstein and Jennifer's father? Epstein felt that her father molded her personality to reflect his own. What effect did this have on Epstein's insecurities?

3) What is the real meaning behind "opposites attract"? Is it true that we all have the possibility to become vulnerable when we allow different individuals into our social circle?

4) Do you think Bruce and Kelly had somewhat of a perfect and open relationship? Would you be able to handle it if your mate shared all of his or her deepest secrets?

5) Can you identify with Jennifer's gregarious, extroverted personality? As such, are you able to justify her uncompromising actions for being controlling and overbearing?

6) Do you think you have the mental power or ability to mold your mate to what you feel he or she should be, as Jennifer thought she'd done with Dr. Epstein?

7) What caused Rodger, the Club's Manager, to kill his wife's lover? Why did Dr. Epstein assume that Jennifer had committed adultery before he looked into the truth?

8) Why does there seem to be such a taboo against men being emotional? Discuss the differences between genders when it comes to talking out and resolving problems.

9) What was Dr. Epstein's obsession with being in love with Jennifer? Did it have more to do with his fear of abandonment or the fact that he was in love with a person that he couldn't control?

10) How do people reconcile being in relationship when they know they're not compatible? Is it better to conceal your thoughts or share them? How long is it possible to sustain the dream that "things will get better"?

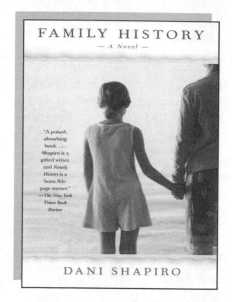

FAMILY HISTORY

Author: Dani Shapiro

Publisher: Anchor Books, 2004

Website: www.readinggroupcenter.com

Available in: Paperback, 288 pages. $13.00 (ISBN 1-4000-3211-3)

Subject: Family Life/ Parenting (Fiction)

Summary

Rachel Jensen is perfectly happy: in love with her husband, devoted to their daughter Kate, gratified by her work restoring art. And finally, she's pregnant again. But as Rachel discovers, perfection can unravel in an instant. The summer she is thirteen, Kate returns from camp sullen, angry, and withdrawn. Everyone assures Rachel it's typical adolescent angst. But then Kate has a terrifying accident with her infant brother, and the ensuing guilt brings forth a dreadful lie—one that ruptures their family, perhaps irrevocably.

Recommended by: *The New York Times Book Review*

"A poised, absorbing book.... Shapiro is a gifted writer, and **Family History** *is a bona fide page-turner."*

Author Biography

Dani Shapiro is the author of three acclaimed novels, **Playing with Fire**, **Fugitive Blue**, and **Picturing the Wreck**, and the best-selling memoir **Slow Motion**. She teaches in the graduate writing program at The New School, and has written for *The New Yorker*, *Granta*, *Elle*, and *Ploughshares*, among other magazines. She lives with her husband and son in Litchfield County, Connecticut.

Topics to Consider

1) The novel is told from Rachel's point of view. Judging from her character as she presents it, is Rachel a good person? What does she want for herself and for her family? What kind of a mother is she?

2) In Dr. Zelman's office, Ned and Rachel are asked for information about their families' psychiatric histories. Rachel admits that her mother has a "narcissistic personality disorder" and begins to feel panic [p. 134]. Judging from her mother's and her daughter's behavior, do Rachel's worries about this possibility seem justified?

3) Why does Ned move out? Does he assume that Rachel believes Kate's accusation that he sexually abused her? How does Ned come across as a father and as a husband?

4) Comment on the novel's structure and on Shapiro's decision to disrupt the narrative chronology. What is the effect of this style on revealing what has happened to the family?

5) *Family History* engages the questions of how we become who we are and how much control we have over our lives, considering our genetic inheritance. Does Rachel worry too much about things she can't possibly control? Or is the problem that a mother can't help but feel that she has to control everything that affects the lives of her family?

6) Judging from Kate's description of the accident on the stairs [pp. 152-164] and her emotional state during the scene at the hospital, does it seem possible that she is concealing the truth about what happened? Or is it clear that what happened was purely accidental? Does this issue remain ambiguous? If so, why?

7) What does the final chapter suggest about the future of the family? Why do Ned and Rachel change their minds and decide to leave Kate at Stone Mountain for a while longer? How hopeful an ending does the novel offer?

For a complete Reading Group Guide, visit
www.readinggroupcenter.com

THE FIVE PEOPLE YOU MEET IN HEAVEN

Author: Mitch Albom

Publisher: Hyperion, 2003

Website: www.hyperionbooks.com

Available in:
Hardcover, 208 pages. $19.95
(ISBN 0-7868-6871-6)

Subject: Identity/
Personal Discovery (Fiction)

Summary

Eddie is a wounded war veteran, an old man who has lived, in his mind, an uninspired life. His job is fixing rides at a seaside amusement park. On his 83rd birthday, a tragic accident kills him as he tries to save a little girl from a falling cart. He awakes in the afterlife, where he learns that heaven is not a destination. It's a place where your life is explained to you by five people, some of whom you knew, others who may have been strangers. One by one, from childhood to soldier to old age, Eddie's five people revisit their connections to him on earth, illuminating the mysteries of his "meaningless" life, and revealing the haunting secret behind the eternal question: "Why was I here?"

Author Biography

Mitch Albom is the author of the #1 international bestseller *Tuesdays with Morrie.* A nationally syndicated columnist for the *Detroit Free Press* and host of a nationally syndicated program for ABC radio, Albom appears regularly on ESPN and has also been named the top sports columnist in the nation 13 times by the Associated Press Sports Editors of America—the highest honor in his field. He is the founder of The Dream Fund, a charity which helps underprivileged youth study art, and of A Time to Help, a volunteer program. Albom serves on the boards of numerous charities. He lives in Michigan with his wife, Janine. Visit **www.AlbomFivePeople.com**.

Topics to Consider

1) What does Albom mean by saying "All endings are also beginnings?" Share something in your life that has begun as another thing ended, and the events that followed.

2) What does Eddie look like? What kind of guy is he? Look at and discuss some of the details and descriptions that paint a picture of Eddie and his place of business. What is it about an amusement park that makes it a good backdrop for this story?

3) How did counting down the final minutes of Eddie's life affect you?

4) What is the significance of Eddie finding himself in the amusement park again after he dies? What is your reaction when Eddie realizes he's spent his entire life trying to get away from Ruby Pier and he is back there immediately after death? Do you think this is important? Why?

5) Describe what Albom's heaven is like. If it differs from what you imagined, share those differences.

6) Even though Eddie hasn't been reincarnated, consider karma in Eddie's life (where actions would affect his reincarnation). If it isn't karma, what is Albom telling us about life and death?

7) Discuss what you might say to Eddie when he laments that he accomplished nothing with his life or when he asks, "Why would heaven make you relive your own decay?"

8) Examine how Eddie's father's choices and decisions actually shape Eddie's life. Share your own experience of a decision your parents made that affected your life, for better or for worse.

9) Briefly recall the five lessons Eddie learns. How might these be important for all of us? Share which five people might meet you in heaven, and what additional or different lessons might be important to your life. How has this story provided a different perspective of your life?

For a complete readers' guide, visit www.hyperionbooks.com

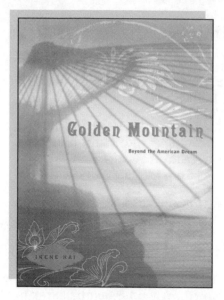

THE GOLDEN MOUNTAIN
Beyond the American Dream

Author: Irene Kai

Publisher: Silver Light, 2004

Website:
www.thegoldenmountain.com

Available in:
Paperback, 368 pages. $14.95
(ISBN 0-9744890-0-X)

Subject: Family Life/
Inspiration (Memoir)

Summary

The true story of four generations of Chinese women who live and die under the restrictions of their culture, except for one: the author, growing up in Hong Kong and transitioning to New York City, she struggled to meld the American dream with her ethnic background. Finally, at age 50, she dares to move into the present and understand the true nature of dreams and what it means to live. She discovered that she didn't have to simply "accept" her fate as her mother and grandmother had done. She could create her own destiny—a destiny filled with passion, vision, and light. This is a deeply inspiring tale of a woman claiming her power.

Recommended by: Professor Dennis P. McCann, Agnes Scott College

"The Golden Mountain draws you in to Irene Kai's daunting journey of spiritual liberation and her struggle to be reconciled with her ancestors, her own self and her family. Those who accept her compelling invitation will soon be launched on their own path toward self-understanding and compassion for others."

Author Biography

Irene Kai was born in Hong Kong and graduated from the School of Visual Arts, NYC and the Royal College of Art, London. Formerly a professor at Penn State University, Irene has traveled extensively and now makes her home in Ashland, Oregon.

Topics to Consider

1) How does Irene break the chain of abusive relationships? Discuss how her experience relates to your life. How does this give you new hope?

2) At the pinnacle of worldly success, Irene Kai arrived at the "American Dream," and decided to walk away—why? What should the American Dream be? Share your dream.

3) Have you ever felt like contemporary culture has typecast you as the victim? Are you sick of feeling anger, sadness, or depression? "We are the only ones who can free ourselves from the victim mentality," says Kai. Discuss how to shatter the shackles that keep us imprisoned.

4) Discover how to openly acknowledge family secrets. Irene learned to forgive by "walking in the shoes" of the women in her family. What are the implications for you and your family? What can you tell others about forgiveness?

5) "We are the masters of our own destiny," says Irene Kai. "When we dare to dream it, we can create it." What is your path to becoming the master of your own destiny?

6) Meditation is but one pathway to freedom from oppression. From Irene's example, discuss what this could mean for you. How can this help you find true love?

7) See the Chinese and American cultures side-by-side. What is the power of cultural influence on us? Discuss the cultural background of your family, for good and ill.

8) How can we be bold and face the common struggles of women in all cultures? Discuss what this means for you and others in your community.

9) For many readers, this has been a "can't put it down" good read. What do you like about this book? How might you now change your life? Discuss how you would begin to tell your personal story.

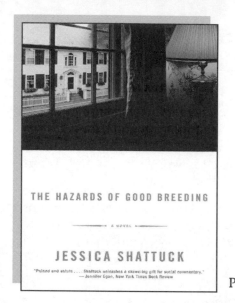

THE HAZARDS OF GOOD BREEDING

Author: Jessica Shattuck

Publisher: W.W. Norton, 2003

Website: www.wwnorton.com

Available in:
Paperback, 304 pages. $13.95
(ISBN 0-393-32483-4)
Hardcover, 288 pages. $23.95
(ISBN 0-393-05132-3)

Subject: Family Life/
Personal Discovery/Identity (Fiction)

Summary

Told from five perspectives, this novel spans an explosive week in the life of the Dunlaps, a WASPy, old-Boston family, and culminates in a series of events that will change their way of life forever. Caroline Dunlap has written off the insular world of debutante parties, golf club luaus, and WASP weddings that she grew up with. But when she reluctantly returns home after her college graduation, she finds that not everything is quite as predictable, or protected, as she had imagined. Her father, Jack, is carrying on stoically after the breakup of his marriage, but he can't stop thinking of Rosita, the family housekeeper he fired almost six months ago. As the real reason for Rosita's departure is revealed, the novel culminates in a series of events that assault the fragile, sheltered, and arguably obsolete world of the Dunlaps.

Recommended by: Newsday

"Will naturally be compared to Cheever's stories and Salinger's Catcher *in the* Rye. *What's more surprising is that it deserves a place beside those masterpieces."*

Author Biography

Jessica Shattuck lives in Cambridge, Massachusetts. Her fiction has been published in *The New Yorker.* She has written nonfiction for *Wired, Mother Jones,* and the *New York Sun.*

Topics to Consider

1) How does Caroline Dunlap change over the course of the novel? How might her choices for post-college life have taken a new direction?

2) Jack Dunlap is an inscrutable man to all who know him. How does Shattuck manage to elicit our sympathy toward him?

3) *The Hazards of Good Breeding* is a comedy of manners with dark undercurrents. How do these come to the surface over the course of the novel? What do they reveal about the Dunlaps' world?

4) Why is Faith Dunlap attracted to Jean Pierre?

5) The novel is very much about people's public fronts versus their interior worlds. How does the theme of role-playing manifest itself throughout the novel?

6) *The Hazards of Good Breeding* is told from five different perspectives. How does this shifting point of view affect our reading of the book and our understanding of the events that unfold?

7) What does Paul Revere's ride embody for Eliot Dunlap?

8) Is Jack in love with Rosita?

9) Describe the role of humor in Shattuck's society portrait. Given that this is in some ways a story about a fragmented family at a moment of crisis, why didn't she choose a more sober tone?

10) What does Caroline realize from her experiences with Stefan?

11) Caroline is initially dismissive of Rock Coughlin. What accounts for her change of heart by the novel's end?

12) How does Shattuck's story relate to a larger portrait of contemporary America?

13) How does *The Hazards of Good Breeding* fit into the American literary tradition of authors like John Cheever and John Updike? What other writers' work does Shattuck's novel call to mind?

14) What are the "hazards of good breeding" in this book?

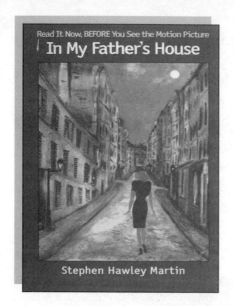

Read It Now, BEFORE You See the Motion Picture
In My Father's House

Stephen Hawley Martin

IN MY FATHER'S HOUSE

Author: Steven Hawley Martin

Publisher: Oaklea Press, 2004

Website: www.OakleaPress.com

Available in:
Hardcover, 252 pages. $24.95
(ISBN 1-892538-12-1)

Subject: Women's Lives/
History/Inspirational (Fiction)

Summary

Fiction and history merge in this fast-paced tale of romantic love, a daughter's devotion, and the supernatural realm of spirit. A 28 year old woman, an early feminist and newspaper reporter from 1952, travels back in time with the help of a voodoo priest to find the cause of the mysterious illness that plunged her father into a coma. She learns more than she bargained for. In Saint Pierre, Martinique, she spends the last few days leading up to May 8, 1902, when at seven in the morning Mt. Pelée erupts with the fury of an atomic bomb. The Little Paris of the Caribbean is completely destroyed, all but one of its 40,000 inhabitants perish, and she learns the secret of life.

Recommended by: *Metaphysical Reviews*

Occasionally, perhaps even rarely, a novel is written that brings together heart-racing action with heart-rending insight. Such is In My Father's House.

Author Biography

Stephen Hawley Martin is the only two-time winner of the *Writer's Digest* Book Award for Fiction, one of which was given for this book which also won him First Prize for Visionary Fiction from *Independent Press*. A former advertising agency president and author of three novels and six non fiction books, he is listed in *Who's Who in the Media and Communications*.

Topics to Consider

1) Do you think Claire was typical of other women her age in 1952? In what ways? How did she differ? Did you find her compassionate or selfish? Giving or judgmental?

2) In many ways, the primary relationship in this novel appears to be between Claire and Jeff. Why do you suppose Claire resists his attempts to get her to commit?

3) The city of St. Pierre Martinique was a disaster waiting to happen in May of 1902. Why do you suppose the governor didn't order its evacuation?

4) Discuss Paul and Angelique's relationship. What forces brought them together, and what forces kept them apart?

5) Claire says her father was a very religious man, though he never tried to force his point of view on her. Why do you suppose he was very religious? Why did he not press his point of view on her? How might it affect someone to have religion forced upon them?

6) Claire journeys into the spirit dimension. What was this like? How was it different from what you would have imagined?

7) Claire believes she discovered the secret of life. Did the secret surprise you? Do you agree with her? Why or why not?

8) Which characters in the book do you feel are the most interesting? Which are the most realistic? Who should play the various parts in the upcoming movie?

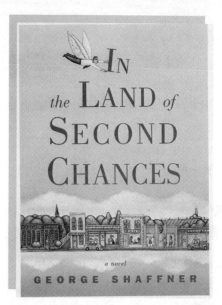

Author: George Shaffner

Publisher: Algonquin, 2004

Website: www.algonquin.com

Available in:
Hardcover, 304 pages. $21.95
(ISBN 1-56512-440-5)

Subject: Americana/
Personal Challenges (Fiction)

Summary

The folks of Ebb, Nebraska have seen their fair share of hardship, but no one more so than Calvin Millet. His wife has left him and his terminally ill young daughter. His department store, the last in the area, is close to bankruptcy. His house has been destroyed by a tornado. Everyone watches Calvin's fortune wane with great interest, for in Ebb, everyone's fate is connected to his. Then Vernon Moore, a traveling salesman with a knack for asking life-altering questions, comes to town. Though Vernon leaves without making a sale, he leaves behind a town where second chances are not only possible; they can—and do—happen.

Recommended by: Phillip Gulley, author, *Harmony* series

"In this humorous and touching tale, George Shaffner does for writing what Louie Armstrong and What a Wonderful World *did for music. A song of a book."*

Author Biography

George Shaffner lives in Sammamish, Washington. He's the author of **The Arithmetic of Life and Death**, which has been described by *American Way* as a "surprising philosophical exploration into how math affects and uncovers truths about our lives." **In the Land of Second Chances** is his first novel.

Topics to Consider

1) Wilma Porter, owner of the Come Again Bed & Breakfast, is the narrator of the story. Why did the author choose to tell the story from her perspective?

2) Discuss how Vernon Moore was received by the various characters in Ebb. Did gender make a difference in how he was viewed and treated?

3) Mr. Moore could have represented other types of products for sale, but the author chose games of chance. Why?

4) Several characters struggled with truth-telling in their lives. Discuss the differences between Calvin sharing the truth directly with Lucy, Mona with her husband and boys, and Clem with Calvin.

5) Vernon often speaks of "reasoned faith" to address the existence of God and an afterlife, instead of traditional religion. What's wrong with conventional "blind" faith, if anything? Why would anyone need "reasoned faith?"

6) When Lucy awakens, Calvin asks her a number of questions. What has he learned from Mr. Moore? What does he learn from Lucy?

7) Was Mr. Moore really a salesman? What did you believe about his past? What did he "sell" the people in the town of Ebb? Discuss how his presence made a difference in their lives and their future.

8) Wilma and Clem acknowledge the presence of Silas the Second. How does the ghost help shape the story?

9) Where is—and what is—the land of second chances?

10) Discuss your feelings about living with uncertainty. Is it truly the spice of life?

11) Has your view of an afterlife changed after reading **In the Land of Second Chances**? If so, what influenced you most?

12) On the final page, we learn that Wilma is taking her time responding to Clem's proposal, and consults Mr. Moore's hand-written message. Do you believe she marries him?

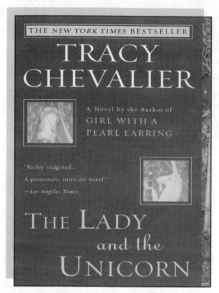

Author: Tracy Chevalier

Publisher: Plume, 2004

Website: www.penguin.com

Available in:
Paperback, 256 pages. $14.00
(ISBN 0-452-28545-3)

Subject: Women's Lives/
Art History (Fiction)

Summary

A tour de force of history and imagination, *The Lady and the Unicorn* is **Tracy Chevalier**'s answer to the mystery behind one of the art world's great masterpieces—a set of bewitching medieval tapestries that hangs today in the Cluny museum in Paris. They appear to portray the seduction of a unicorn, but the story behind their making is unknown—until now. In *The Lady and the Unicorn*, **Tracy Chevalier** weaves fact and fiction into a beautiful, timeless, and intriguing literary tapestry—an extraordinary story exquisitely told.

Recommended by: *The New York Times Book Review*

"Subtly rendered, surprisingly complex characters...a novel notable for its human warmth."

Author Biography

Tracy Chevalier is the author of the best-selling *Girl With a Pearl Earring*, a favorite selection of book groups. An American originally from Washington, D.C., she now lives in London with her husband and son.

Topics to Consider

1) The novel is structured around the making of the tapestries, from their conception to their completion. The lives of the people involved in their creation are altered. What does this suggest about the interconnectedness of life and art?

2) Each character has a different understanding of the function of art. Is it, as Claude believes "to imitate life" or is it as Nicolas des Innocents suggests, "to make things more beautiful than they are?"

3) The novel is written from a number of points of view. What does this allow Tracy Chevalier to achieve? Nicolas des Innocents's point of view is pivotal. Can you explain why?

4) Is Nicolas des Innocents as innocent as his name suggests? What does he learn by the end of the novel?

5) The tapestries feature a unicorn and a lady. In the novel, a unicorn is a symbol that has a very different meaning for each character. What does the unicorn represent to Nicolas des Innocents? To Jean LeViste? What else does the unicorn mean?

6) How are secrets important in this novel?

7) How is the relationship between Claude and Genevieve different from the relationship between Alienor and Christine? How are they similar? What do they suggest about the way mothers and daughters interacted with each other at this point in time?

8) What was the primary role of women at this point in history? How did the novel's different women deal with the limitations placed upon them by society?

9) How does Philippe de la Tour's job as the cartoonist foreshadow the part he will play in Alienor's life?

For a complete reading group guide, visit www.penguin.com

LEAH'S WAY

Author: Richard Botelho

Publisher: Windstream, 2004

Website: www.LeahsWay.com

Available in:
Paperback, 256 pages. $12.95
(ISBN 0-9643926-9-0)

Subject: Women's Lives/
Inspiration and Faith (Fiction)

Summary

Leah's Way is an intriguing story of one woman's journey through life and her search to find justification and love. It is also the story of the human quest for meaning, embodied in a character who experiences the full spectrum of our fallibility and resolve. By clinging to her essence, Leah demonstrates how the often confusing duality of this world can be both understood and overcome, and the purpose of life itself revealed.

Recommended by: *Library Journal*

"Botelho's heartrending and convincing account reinforces just how fragile our worlds can be."

Author Biography

Richard Brian Botelho, who lives in Danville, CA, is a recognized professional writer, marketing consultant, economic analyst, and social philosopher since 1984. He is frequently interviewed by both local and national media for his opinions on matters as diverse as economic policy, consumer behavior, societal trends, and global integration. His book, *The New Individualism: Personal Change to Transform Society*, is used in over 100 colleges and universities. This is his first novel.

Topics to Consider

1) What is it about the Mother/Father relationship that appears to be so difficult? Why does Walton allow Margaret to treat him with such disrespect? Why does Margaret feel the way she does and how do her feelings change over time?

2) Is Margaret justified in being so harsh with Leah? What is her motivation? Why does Walton not intervene?

3) Blake was Leah's first love. Was she too young and inexperienced? Why couldn't she let herself get past him? In her mind, does the relationship become more than it ever was?

4) Margaret whips Leah for getting a "C" in chemistry. Is the whipping really about a "C"? How realistic is it for Leah to think that a Christian College would help her find herself and safeguard her beliefs?

5) Leah sees Vic as her ticket out of Nashville. What was Leah searching for by escaping Nashville? How does her faith sustain her at this time?

6) Leah feels she <u>should</u> be happy but melancholy seems to follow her. Her father is gone, she is frustrated and full of self-pity and bitterness; she is in marital hell. Was her affair with Dan inevitable?

7) What about David? He is unforgiving and disowns his mother. Do you think his feelings and actions are justified?

8) After the divorce and over a period of time Leah meets other men but does not have a satisfactory relationship. Jay tells her she is incapable of loving anyone. Do you think that is so? Roberto tells her she must trust in life and dare to take a chance. Why is this such a hard thing for her to do?

9) Do you think Leah's choice to wander the country is meant as self-punishment? What is she looking for?

10) Life brings all of us some degree of pain and disappointment. Why could Leah not accept this as part of her life adventure?

LONG DAY'S JOURNEY INTO NIGHT

Author: Eugene O'Neill

Publisher: Yale University Press

Website: www.yalebooks.com

Available in:
Paperback, 180 pages, $12.95
(ISBN 0-300-09305-5)

Subject: Family Life/
Relationships (Fiction)

Summary

Eugene O'Neill's autobiographical play is regarded as his finest work. First published in 1956, it won the Pulitzer Prize in 1957 and has since sold more than one million copies. This edition includes a new foreword by Harold Bloom, who writes: "The helplessness of family love to sustain, let alone heal, the wounds of marriage, of parenthood, and of sonship, have never been so remorselessly and so pathetically portrayed, and with a force of gesture too painful ever to be forgotten by any of us."

Recommended by: José Quintero

"Only an artist of O'Neill's extraordinary skill and perception can draw the curtain on the secrets of his own family to make you peer into your own. [This play] is the most remarkable achievement of one of the world's greatest dramatists."

Author Biography

Eugene O'Neill (1888-1953), the father of American drama, began writing plays in 1913, and by 1916 his one-act play *Bound East for Cardiff* was produced in New York. In 1920 his full-length play *Beyond the Horizon* was produced and won O'Neill the first of his four Pulitzer Prizes. Over the next few decades, O'Neill published 24 other full-length plays. After receiving the Nobel Prize for literature in 1936, he published two of his most highly acclaimed plays, *The Iceman Cometh* and *A Moon for the Misbegotten*. **Long Day's Journey Into Night** was published three years after his death.

Topics to Consider

1) Discuss O'Neill's use of stage directions. How does the language employed by O'Neill in his directions differ from that spoken by the characters? How do these directions serve to deepen our understanding of action and characters?

2) How does O'Neill conceive of the possibilities of American life? Marriage? Parenthood?

3) How do dreams function to deepen our understanding of the characters? Are any of the characters' dreams attained or attainable?

4) Discuss the issue of substance abuse in the play. What role does it play in the lives of parents and children?

5) Consider the topic of lying. Who lies to whom, when, and for what reasons? Is anyone honest in the play? When?

6) Discuss the subject of monotony—in what the characters do and say, and in the play's setting.

7) Consider the topic of fathers and sons. What kind of relationship does Tyrone have with his two sons? What is the source of the conflict between generations?

MEDICINE, MIND AND MEANING

Author: Eve A. Wood, MD

Publisher: In One Press, 2004

Website: www.InOnePress.com

Available in:
Hardcover, 347 pages. $21.95
(ISBN 0-9741083-0-8)

Subject: Identity/
Personal Triumph (Nonfiction)

Summary

It's been said that the shortest distance between two people is a story. Like many novels woven into one volume, psychiatrist Eve Wood and her patients share captivating and miraculous tales that show how life can be enriched and fulfilling even though we experience times of frustration, loss, illness, and other personal crises. While posing universal questions: *Who am I?*, *What do I think?*, and *Why am I here?*, Wood combines her professional knowledge about healing and wellness with valuable and true stories. What results is a compassionate, thought-filled, and encouraging book filled with wisdom meant to enrich life's journey with better understanding, clarity, and purpose. It prompts us to consider the importance of telling our own stories and listening to the stories of others.

Recommended by: C. Everett Koop, MD

"I have seldom been so moved by a book."

Author Biography

Eve A. Wood, MD, has been helping individuals from all walks of life grow through their experiences. She has served on the faculty of Univ. of Pennsylvania School of Medicine and recently been appointed Clinical Associate Professor of Medicine at the University of Arizona Program in Integrative Medicine. Her work has attracted attention and acclaim from the nation's leading authorities in the fields of medicine, health and spiritual well-being.

Topics to Consider

1) The three-legged stool is used as a symbol for life, wellness, and healing. Discuss the value of this symbol in helping you understand the critical elements of your body, mind and spirit for healthy living.

2) Discuss the role of forgiveness in healing and growth. At what point is forgiveness possible?

3) Discuss your response to Gillie's story. Do you know anyone who has struggled so much with daily life? Why was Gillie able to pull her life together? Will Gillie ever fully conquer her challenges? Do any of us?

4) Dr. Wood says, "Your gifts outweigh all of your shortcomings and vulnerabilities. You are *meant* to heal." Why do you believe she felt so strongly about stating this in the book?

5) Do most of us understand the difference between thoughts and feelings? How is this distinction pivotal to our relationships with others?

6) Discuss the value of looking back at childhood experiences to put life in context. Can personal growth take place without examining the past? What revelations from this process have you experienced that have allowed you to gain better understanding of yourself?

7) Liza and Shari both experienced wrong fits...jobs that did not fit who they were. How does one recognize a "wrong fit" and then work toward finding the "right fit?"

8) The book closes with the words of Dr. Wood's patients. What was accomplished with these stories—for the patients themselves, for Dr. Wood, and for readers? Discuss how telling our stories—and listening to the stories of others—can transform our lives. What stories have most influenced you?

Eve Wood invites you to contact her to meet with your group by speaker phone. You can reach her by visiting www.InOnePress.com.

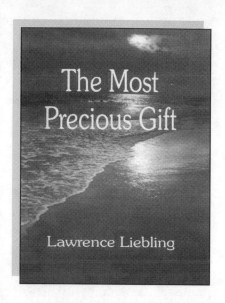

Author: Lawrence Liebling

Publisher: Silent River Press

Available in:
Hardcover, 215 pages, $19.95
(ISBN 0-9642874-2-0)

Subject: Family Life/Personal
Challenges/Relationships (Memoir)

Summary

What would you do if someone close to you was about to die unless you put your own life on the line? There is a moment in every person's life that has the power to be so defining that it changes the lens through which he or she sees the world. For author Lawrence Liebling, that moment occurs in 1974 when his sister, gravely ill for four years, is desperately in need of a new and risky medical procedure, a kidney transplant. At the age of 20, he is asked to be the donor and he consents. The operation is a success, but the immediate results hide unforeseen consequences. This true story follows relationships over the span of the next 25 years, as they twist and turn down a path of joy and celebration, as well as hardship and tragedy.

Recommended by: Charles Klein, author

"This book powerfully reminds us what a precious gift we are to each other, and teaches us never to take both life and the people we share it with for granted."

Author Biography

For the past 25 years, **Lawrence Liebling** owned and operated a highly specialized electronics company based in New York. More recently he has edited and published several books including the critically acclaimed *How to Forgive When You Can't Forget*, by Charles Klein. Mr. Liebling lives in Long Island, New York with his wife, Carolyn, and son, Josh, and golden retriever, Molly.

Topics to Consider

1) Risking your life for someone you love may seem like a given, at least in theory. If put to the test, however, such a decision—if some thought were required rather than an instinctive response—could be filled with many nuances and complications. Discuss some of the considerations one might have in making such a critical decision.

2) Several books have been published over the years, such as **Why Bad Things Happen to Good People** and **How to Forgive When You Can't Forget**, that address why some of us are forced to endure great hardship and others not. How have you personally reconciled the answers to these perplexing questions?

3) Larry and Debbie's parents decide to withhold the truth about the seriousness of her disease. What was their motivation? Would you have done the same?

4) Liebling writes, "Life gives us moments where we can step forward and change a result, and that by doing so we change ourselves." Cite some examples of how this might be true.

5) Discuss the point at which "What if?" ceases to be hopeful and inventive, and becomes paralyzing instead.

6) What are your thoughts about the passage of time in this story: the full day Liebling spends lost in reflection, a few months after his sister's death, 20+ years after the event that formed the basis for this book?

7) Liebling's story points out how awkward and difficult it can be to find the right words to say under certain circumstances. Have you ever experienced such a moment? How did you deal with it? What would you suggest others do or say to convey comfort or support?

8) Gifts are abundant in many family relationships—from tangible presents to the gift of love. What would each member of Liebling's family have claimed to be their "most precious gift?" Which do you suppose might have been most precious to the author: knowing that his sacrifice saved his sister's life, or to be acknowledged and thanked for said sacrifice?

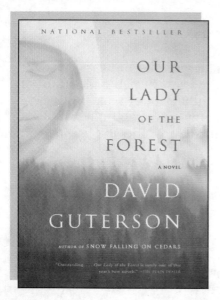

OUR LADY OF THE FOREST

Author: David Guterson

Publisher: Vintage Books, 2004

Website:
www.readinggroupcenter.com

Available in:
Paperback, 336 pages. $13.00
(ISBN 0-375-72657-8)

Subject: Americana/
Inspiration & Faith (Fiction)

Summary

From **David Guterson**—bestselling author of *Snow Falling on Cedars*—comes this emotionally charged, provocative novel about what happens when a fifteen-year-old girl becomes an instrument of divine grace. Ann Holmes is a fragile, pill-popping teenaged runaway who receives a visitation from the Virgin Mary one morning while picking mushrooms in the woods of North Fork, Washington. In the ensuing days the miracle recurs, and the declining logging town becomes the site of a pilgrimage of the faithful and desperate. As these people flock to Ann—and as Ann herself is drawn more deeply into what is either holiness or madness—*Our Lady of the Forest* seamlessly splices the miraculous and the mundane.

Recommended by: *The Plain Dealer*

"Outstanding.... **Our Lady of the Forest** *is surely one of this year's best novels.*"

Author Biography

David Guterson is the author of the novels *East of the Mountains* and *Snow Falling on Cedars*, and of a collection of short stories, *The Country Ahead of Us, the Country Behind*. A Guggenheim Fellow and a PEN/Faulkner Award winner, he lives in Washington State.

Topics to Consider

1) The book's opening echoes the tone of official reportage, using "the girl" instead of naming Ann Holmes. Elsewhere in the narrative Ann is called "the visionary." Why? Does this create a sense of distance from her?

2) What role do sexuality and sexual desire play in this story, particularly for Tom Cross, Father Collins, and Ann? What attracts Father Collins to Ann [p. 38]? Are beauty, sexual desire, violence, and victimization interrelated in this novel? If so, how?

3) Does Guterson expect his readers to believe that Ann's encounters with the Virgin Mary are real? Does he seem sympathetic to the position of Father Collins, who is skeptical and yet open-minded, or of Carolyn, who is entirely analytical and cynical about the visions? Is there a character with whom readers are most likely to identify? Who is it?

4) What kind of person is Carolyn Greer? Is she an opportunist, an intellectual, a cynic, an actor, a thief? If she is talented and intelligent, why is she living in a campground in North Fork? Is she a more intriguing character than Ann?

5) The narrator shares with readers the information that Ann is a victim of violent sexual abuse; this fact is not made known, however, to Father Collins or to the public, and so it is not a factor in the inquiry into her case. What are the effects on the reader of knowing Ann's history?

6) What are readers to make of the thousands of believers who come to North Fork to follow Ann to the site of her visions? What does Guterson suggest about the psychology of large groups and the behavior of crowds [pp. 136-148]?

7) What are the dynamics of the scene in which Tom Cross confronts Ann in the church [pp. 300-310]? What does Tom Cross want from Ann, and how close to violence is he? Why does Carolyn intervene as she does?

For a complete Reading Group Guide, visit
www.readinggroupcenter.com

THE PHOTOGRAPH

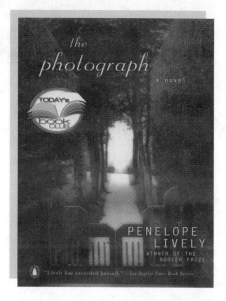

Author: Penelope Lively

Publisher: Penguin Books, 2004

Website: www.penguin.com

Available in:
Paperback, 240 pages. $14.00
(ISBN 0-14-200442-1)

Subject: Relationships/
Personal Discovery (Fiction)

Summary

It opens with a snapshot: Kath, at an unknown gathering, hands clasped with a man not her husband. The photograph is in an envelope marked DON'T OPEN—DESTROY. But Kath's husband does not heed the warning. The mystery of the photograph, and of Kath's recent death, propels him on a journey of discovery in which he must peel back layers of their lives. The unfolding tale reveals a tight web of secrets—within marriages, between two sisters, and at the heart of an affair. Kath, with her mesmerizing looks and casual ways, moves like a ghost through the thoughts and memories of everyone who knew her.

Recommended by: *The Atlantic Monthly*

"Original...bracingly intelligent. Rarely has a subject as elusive as life's messiness been pursued with such unflagging rigor."

Author Biography

Penelope Lively grew up in Egypt but settled in England after the war. She is the author of many prize-winning novels and short story collections for both adults and children. Lively has twice been shortlisted for the Booker Prize, and won the award in 1987 for her highly acclaimed novel *Moon Tiger*. She lives in Oxfordshire and London.

Topics to Consider

1) Expecting to find further infidelities, what harsher truths, about himself as well as Kath, does Glyn uncover? In what ways does he need to learn these things? In what ways does his professional life suit him to his search?

2) Why does Lively tell the story from different points of view? In what ways are multiple perspectives appropriate to the nature of the story?

3) In what ways do the characters in the novel use and distort the reality of who Kath was to "fit" their narratives? Does the narrative of the novel itself give Kath her own "voice"?

4) In what ways is the novel as a whole about not only how the past changes the present but how the present changes the past?

5) Kath is forever intruding into people's thoughts, rising up before them unbidden. Why does her absent presence have such power for the characters who survived her? In what ways did the absent presences of her own unborn children affect the course and outcome of her life?

6) To what extent is Glyn, in his inability to listen and to know Kath, responsible for her death? What crucial things about Kath does he fail to understand? Why was he unable to listen fully to her when she was alive? Did he really love her?

7) In what sense is Kath's beauty both a privilege and a curse?

8) How surprising is it to learn the reasons for Kath's suicide? Do these reasons seem in keeping with her character? Why were none of the people who knew her best able to see that she was in danger?

9) What does the novel suggest about our ability to know each other? What does it suggest about the role listening plays in such relationships?

For a complete reader's guide, visit www.penguin.com

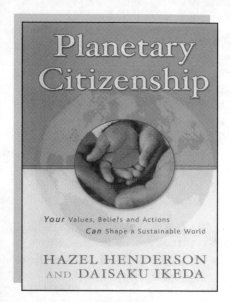

PLANETARY CITIZENSHIP

Author: Hazel Henderson,
Daisaku Ikeda

Publisher: Middleway Press, 2004

Website: www.middlewaypress.org

Available in:
Hardcover, 186 pages. $23.95
(ISBN 0-9723267-2-3)

Subject: Culture & World Issues/
Social Issues (Nonfiction)

Summary

Two world-renowned global activists explore the rise of "grassroots globalists"—citizens all over the world who are taking responsibility to build a more peaceful, harmonious and sustainable future. A wide variety of issues are explored, including economic justice, democratizing politics, making corporations accountable, and conserving the Earth's biodiversity. Complex global issues are linked to ordinary people, assuring us that we have the power to make a positive difference in our families, communities, countries and the world at large.

Recommended by: Barbara Marx Hubbard

[Henderson and Ikeda] "...reveal a vital blueprint for a compassionate and sustainable world ... and make a formidable team stepping forward as humanity's guides in this great transition to the next stage of social evolution."

Author Biography

Hazel Henderson, author of eight other books, is a world-renowned futurist, evolutionary economist, globally syndicated columnist and consultant on sustainable development. **Daisaku Ikeda** is president of the Soka Gakkai International, a lay Buddhist association promoting peace, culture and education. He is recognized as one of the world's leading interpreters of Buddhism.

Topics to Consider

1) The book is written in dialogue format. How would your experience of reading the book be different if the concepts were instead presented in typical narrative manner?

2) How do Henderson and Ikeda model the process of dialogue? How does their dialogue differ from what we usually hear and see on radio and television programs?

3) Discuss the childhood experiences of Henderson and Ikeda. How was their concern for the world inspired by others? Who in your life has encouraged you to look beyond your own needs?

4) What is your view of the escalating acts of hostility and violence the world now faces? Are they steps backwards or opportunities for enlightenment? Discuss the range of possible outcomes from times of intense conflict.

5) Is it necessary to experience success over adversity on a personal level before being able to see it as a possibility for the world?

6) Discuss how the use of professionals, so-called experts, and even not-for-profit institutes by politicians and the media has changed over the years. What qualified, neutral and credible sources of research and advice have you discovered to be trustworthy in today's world?

7) What advice would you give a young person on what kind of education is worth pursuing for achieving a good living and a good life?

8) If a worldwide poll was taken of ordinary people, how many do you believe would agree with Henderson that "the real 'axis of evil' we must overcome consists of poverty, ignorance, disease and violence?" Can you envision a tipping point that would help us make progress?

9) Henderson suggests, "We must realize that when basic needs have been met, human development is primarily about *being* more, not *having* more." What evidence is there to support the idea that this shift is taking place?

10) What are the obstacles to giving women basic human rights in some areas of the world? What might be the most effective path for influencing this change?

PS, I LOVE YOU

Author: Cecilia Ahern

Publisher: Hyperion, 2004

Website: www.hyperionbooks.com

Available in:
Paperback (1/05), 480 pages. $13.95
(ISBN 0-7868-9075-4)
Hardcover, 375 pages. $21.95
(ISBN 1-4013-0090-1)

Subject: Relationships/
Personal Triumph (Fiction)

Summary

Holly couldn't live without her husband Gerry, until the day she had to. They were the kind of young couple who could finish each other's sentences. When Gerry succumbs to a terminal illness and dies, 30-year-old Holly is set adrift, unable to pick up the pieces. But with the help of a series of letters her husband left her before he died and a little nudging from an eccentric assortment of family and friends, she learns to laugh, overcome her fears, and discover a world she never knew existed.

Recommended by: Marian Keyes

"Sweet and sad and funny: a charming journey from grief to hope."

Author Biography

Cecelia Ahern, the 22-year old daughter of Ireland's prime minister, Bertie Ahern, holds a degree in Journalism and Media Communications and was studying for a master's degree in film when she decided to leave school and write her first novel. She lives in Dublin.

Topics to Consider

1) Keeping in mind that Ahern was 21 when she wrote *PS, I Love You*, discuss her strengths as a storyteller. How effective is she at describing Holly's experiences? If you have lost a loved one, or know someone who has, discuss how much you relate to Holly's mourning process.

2) Briefly describe Holly's family and friends. Which characters do you like most? Why?

3) How does the idea of "a list" come about? What is so compelling about a list left by a loved one who has died? How does the list help Holly? Talk about which item was the most difficult for her, and why. If you know anyone who has been left such a list, share how it affected them.

4) Looking at Gerry's letter to Holly in the package with the envelopes/list, discuss what you felt while reading it. Why does Holly feel both sad and relieved?

5) Even though Gerry is dead, how does he come alive in the book? At what point in the book do we learn the most about Gerry? Describe him both physically and mentally.

6) Discuss the personal transformations in *PS, I Love You*. Why is it important that we see the characters moving on? Who is Holly at the book's start, and at the book's end?

7) What is some of the evidence that shows Holly moving on? Why does Holly cool towards Jack? How do Sharon's pregnancy and Denise's marriage help Holly?

8) How does Ahern set up Holly's relationship with Daniel? Did you think Holly was going to hook up with Daniel? Why? Discuss what happens in Daniel's love life, and why he makes the choice he does.

9) The garden is one of many metaphors that Ahern uses in *PS, I Love You*. What are some others? How do these metaphors enrich the story? How do they amplify Holly's journey?

For a complete reader's guide, visit www.hyperionbooks.com

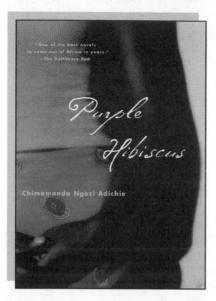

PURPLE HIBISCUS

Author:
Chimamanda Ngozi Adichie

Publisher: Anchor Books, 2004

Website:
www.readinggroupcenter.com

Available in:
Paperback, 320 pages. $13.00
(ISBN 1-4000-7694-3)

Subject: Family Life/Culture &
World Issues (Fiction)

Summary

Fifteen-year-old Kambili's world is circumscribed by the high walls and frangipani trees of her family compound. Her wealthy Catholic father, under whose shadow Kambili lives, while generous and politically active in the community, is repressive and fanatically religious at home. When Nigeria begins to fall apart under a military coup, Kambili's father sends her and her brother away to stay with their aunt, a University professor, whose house is noisy and full of laughter. There, Kambili and her brother discover a life and love beyond the confines of their father's authority. The visit will lift the silence from their world and, in time, give rise to devotion and defiance that reveal themselves in profound and unexpected ways.

Recommended by: *The Baltimore Sun*

"One of the best novels to come out of Africa in years."

Author Biography

Chimamanda Ngozi Adichie grew up in Nigeria, where she attended medical school for two years at the University of Nigeria before coming to the United States. An O. Henry Prize winner, Adichie was shortlisted for the Caine Prize for African Writing. Her work has appeared in various literary publications, including *Zoetrope* and the *Iowa Review*. She now divides her time between the United States and Nigeria.

Topics to Consider

1) What is the emotional atmosphere in Kambili's home? What effect does this have on Kambili and Jaja? Why is their father so strict?

2) When Kambili visits Aunty Ifeoma, she is immediately struck by how much laughter fills the house. Why is it so surprising to her to hear people speak, laugh, and argue so freely? How does she manage to regain her own ability to speak, and, most importantly, to laugh?

3) Amaka says, "Uncle Eugene is not a bad man, really. . . . People have problems, people make mistakes" [p. 251]. Is he in fact a "bad man"? Why does he violently abuse his wife and children? What good deeds does he perform? How can his generosity and political integrity coexist with his religious intolerance?

4) In what ways are Aunty Ifeoma and Eugene different from one another? How does each character approach life? How do they differ in their religious views? Why is Ifeoma so much happier even though she is poor and her brother is rich?

5) Why does Kambili's mother keep returning to her husband, even after he beats her so badly that he causes a miscarriage, and even after he nearly kills Kambili? How does she justify her husband's behavior? How should she be judged for poisoning her husband?

6) What does the novel as a whole say about the nature of religion? About the relationship between belief and behavior?

7) What does **Purple Hibiscus** reveal about life in Nigeria? How are Nigerians similar to Americans? In what significant ways are they different? How do Americans regard Nigerians in the novel?

8) Why does Adichie end the novel with an image of rain clouds? What are the implications of Kambili feeling that the clouds hung so low she "could reach out and squeeze the moisture from them?" What is the meaning of the novel's very simple final sentence: "The new rains will come down soon?"

For a complete Reading Group Guide, visit
www.readinggroupcenter.com

READING GROUP CHOICES   53

THE READING GROUP

Author: **Elizabeth Noble**

Publisher: Perennial (Jan. '05)

Website: www.harpercollins.com

Available in:
Paperback, 480 pages. $14.95
(ISBN 0-060-76044-3)

Subject: Women's Lives/
Friendship (Fiction)

Summary

What starts out as a good idea born from a glass of wine and the need to socialize turns into much more. Over the span of a year, Clare, Harriet, Nicole, Polly and Susan—five women of different ages, backgrounds and contrasting dilemmas—transform themselves through the shared community of a book group. Their reading group becomes a forum for each of the women's views, expressed initially by the book they're reading and increasingly openly as the bonds of friendship cement. As the months pass, these women's lives become more and more intertwined. In **The Reading Group**, Noble reveals the many complicated paths in life we all face as well as the power and importance of friendship.

Recommended by: *Choice* **(London)**

"A lively, witty novel that touches on themes of friendship and the redemptive power of art."

Author Biography

Elizabeth Noble lives in Guildford, Surrey with her husband and two daughters. *The Reading Group* is her first novel.

Topics to Consider

1) There are many female protagonists in **The Reading Group**. What does each contribute personality-wise to the overall reading group?

2) What two characters change the course of their lives the most throughout the book?

3) Harriet and Nicole are best friends. What are the differences and similarities in their relationships with their husbands?

4) Polly has had to make personal sacrifices as a single mother. When her daughter Cressida gets pregnant, why does she decide that she should raise the baby?

5) Susan and her sister Margaret could not be more different with how they each have dealt with the loss of their mother to dementia—how do they both reconcile their pain for their mother and their own relationship?

6) How does the fiction the group chooses to read relate to the reality of their lives?

7) Have you ever hosted a reading group? What would you do differently than the women in Elizabeth Noble's book?

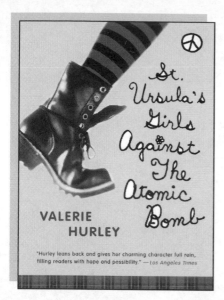

"Hurley leans back and gives her charming character full rein, filling readers with hope and possibility." — *Los Angeles Times*

ST. URSULA'S GIRLS AGAINST THE ATOMIC BOMB

Author: Valerie Hurley

Publisher: Plume, 2004

Website: www.penguin.com

Available in:
Paperback, 272 pages. $13.00
(ISBN 0-452-28569-0)

Subject: Women's Lives/Faith/
Personal Discovery (Fiction)

Summary

Raine Rassaby, a senior at St. Ursula's Academy in New York City, is frustrated with the annoying requirements for school—and with being Catholic, so she converts to Judaism and attends school with the Star of David painted on her fingernails. Rather than study, Raine organizes a group called St. Ursula's Girls Against the Atomic Bomb. Hoping to set Raine on a more wholesome path, the Mother Superior sends her to the school guidance counselor, Al Klepatar. In the depths of their fractured worlds, Raine and Al are surprised by what they discover—about the world and about themselves.

Recommended by: Karen Joy Fowler, author,
The Jane Austen Book Club

"Lucky you, reading it for the first time."

Author Biography

Valerie Hurley won the *Indiana Review* Fiction prize, and has published stories in *The Iowa Review, The Missouri Review, The North American Review,* and *New Letters,* among others. Two of her essays have appeared in *The Best American Essays* anthologies. She lives in Vermont with her husband.

Topics to Consider

1) What is compelling and different about Al, the other protagonist of the novel? How does he serve as a sort of narrator for the events in Raine's life, and yet work as a character himself?

2) What do Raine's journal entries tell us about Raine herself, and the people that surround her?

3) Discuss the progression of Al's relationship with Raine. At what point does it shift from a student/counselor dynamic to something resembling friendship? Discuss the positive and negative effects that this friendship has on both of their lives.

4) Discuss Al's faith in himself, in his marriage, and in his work. How does this kind of faith differ from religious faith? What role does religious faith play in the novel, and what purpose does it serve?

5) Discuss Al's relationship with his wife Frieda. Is there a gradual disintegration of their relationship, or is the marriage already over by the time the book begins? What does Al learn about his relationships and his daily interaction with other people, let alone his wife, through the breakup of his marriage?

6) Discuss Raine's epiphany regarding Pavel. At what moment does it truly arrive—when they're on the bus in Nebraska, or when she tells him that she's pregnant? Discuss Pavel's reaction to the news of Raine's pregnancy. How unexpected is his response?

7) Discuss the shift that takes place in the novel once Al and Raine move out to the farmhouse in upstate New York. What kind of changes do Al and Raine go through, and how significant are these changes?

8) To what extent have Raine and Al "transformed" over the course of the book? What can the reader expect for these characters, and for their futures? Is there one shining, clear, redeeming moral lesson at the book's end? Or is there a more complex message at the end of the novel?

For a complete reading group guide, visit www.penguin.com

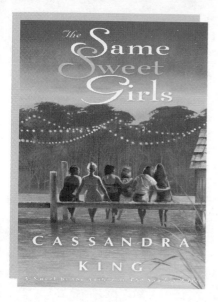

THE SAME SWEET GIRLS

Author: Cassandra King

Publisher: Hyperion, 2004

Website: www.hyperionbooks.com

Available in:
Hardcover, 416 pages. $23.95
(ISBN 1-4013-0038-3)

Subject: Women's Lives/
Friendship (Fiction)

Summary

None of the Same Sweet Girls are really girls anymore and none of them have actually ever been that sweet. But this spirited group of Southern women, who have been holding biannual reunions ever since they were together in college, are nothing short of compelling. There's Julia Stovall, the First Lady of Alabama, who, despite her public veneer, is a down-to-earth gal who only wants to know who her husband is sneaking out with late at night. There's Lanier Sanders, whose husband won custody of their children after he found out about her fling with a colleague. Then there's Astor Deveaux, a former Broadway showgirl who simply can't keep her flirtations in check. And Corinne Cooper, whose incredible story comes to light as the novel unfolds.

Recommended by: Ann Rivers Siddons

"If anybody has written a better book about the power of women's friendships, I haven't read it. I really, truly love this book."

Author Biography

Cassandra King is a native of Alabama, where she formerly taught English and creative writing classes. Her previous novels include **The Sunday Wife** and **Making Waves**. She currently resides in South Carolina with her husband, Pat Conroy, and she belongs to a real-life Same Sweet Girls group, which reunites every year.

Topics to Consider

1) Look at the Walt Whitman quote at the beginning of **The Same Sweet Girls**. Why does King use this here?

2) Why does Corrine state early on that, "The illusion of sweetness, that's all that counts...Southern girls will stab you in the back, same as anyone else, but we'll give you a sugary smile while doing it?" Why is this important to the story?

3) Briefly describe each of the Same Sweet Girls. Share your impression of the group. Who do you like the most, and why? What are their backgrounds? How did they become a group, and why are they such good friends?

4) Why are characters like Astor and Roseanelle accepted and tolerated, even loved, by the rest of the group? How do they influence other characters in the book? Why do others accept and even ignore such obvious flaws in their friends?

5) What kind of relationships do these SSGs have with the men in their lives? What about the SSGs relationships with men reveals, or possibly reflects, their views of themselves?

6) Recount Julia's relationship with her mother. What was her mother's reaction when Bethany was born? Did Julia somehow agree with her mother? How does Julia evolve, and what enables her to do so?

7) Trace Corrine's personal history. Why is she the one who has a terminal disease? What does Miles mean when he says to her, "Your biography becomes your biology?"

8) Why is Cal so attracted to Corrine? What is significant about the timing of his interest? What is the significance of the large kettle gourd that he returns to her? What enables his aged grandmother to understand the purpose of this kettle gourd?

9) What is symbolic about Corrine giving the other SSGs a gourd seed?

10) What resonates, and affects you the most, about **The Same Sweet Girls**? What stays with you?

For a complete reader's guide, visit www.hyperionbooks.com

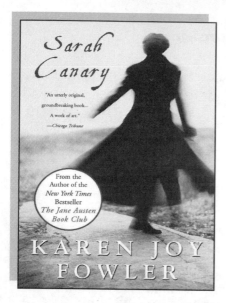

SARAH CANARY

Author: Karen Joy Fowler

Publisher: Plume Books, 2003

Website: www.penguin.com

Available in:
Paperback, 304 pages. $14.00
(ISBN 0-452-28647-6)

Subject: Women's Lives/
American History (Fiction)

Summary

When black-cloaked Sarah Canary wanders into a railway camp in the Washington territories in 1873, Chin Ah Kin is ordered by his uncle to escort "the ugliest woman he could imagine" away. Far away. But Chin soon becomes the follower. In the first of many such instances, they are separated, both resurfacing some days later at an insane asylum. Chin has run afoul of the law and Sarah has been committed for observation. Their escape from the asylum in the company of another inmate sets into motion a series of adventures and misadventures that are at once hilarious, deeply moving, and downright terrifying.

Recommended by: *The Washington Post Book World*

"Powerfully imagined...Drop everything and follow Sarah Canary... Humor and horror, history and myth dance cheek to cheek in this Jack London meets L. Frank Baum world."

Author Biography

Karen Joy Fowler, a PEN/Faulkner finalist and Dublin IMPAC nominee, is the author of the *New York Times* bestseller **The Jane Austen Book Club** and the *New York Times* Notable Books **Sister Noon, The Sweetheart Season,** and **Black Glass: Short Fictions.** She lives in Davis, California.

Topics to Consider

1) One of the themes of **Sarah Canary** is how perception shapes reality. Chin, Adelaide, B.J., and Harold have vastly different views when it comes to the identity of Sarah Canary. Given this, why do you think Karen Joy Fowler leaves the question of Sarah Canary's identity a mystery?

2) Why do you think Fowler has intertwined her narrative with short chapters of actual events from the nineteenth century?

3) **Sarah Canary** is set in the Washington Territory in the 1870s, just after the American Civil War. From a historical and geographic standpoint, what is the significance of this setting for **Sarah Canary**?

4) Chin talks about the one-winged bird and Burke talks about nature loving symmetry. Is it also human nature to condemn something that is different or irregular? Why?

5) What does Tom mean when he says, "The earth talks to us, but we don't speak its language. Why should it not mean something just because you don't understand?"

6) The last chapter of the book reports recent news events—Jim Bakker's fall from grace, the massacre in Tiananmen Square, President Reagan's politically incorrect speech about the plight of the American Indian, etc. Why do you think the author ends the book this way?

7) The main characters in **Sarah Canary**—a Chinese railway worker, a suffragist, an escaped mental patient, and a huckster—are all considered outcasts of the age. Who are their modern equivalents and how do their experiences differ from those of people who have been marginalized in the past?

8) In the end, what do each of the characters gain as a result of their journey in pursuit of Sarah Canary? Are the characters better off for their experience?

9) Why is the story of Sarah Canary narrated by someone of the late twentieth century?

THE SECRET LIFE OF BEES

Author: Sue Monk Kidd

Publisher: Penguin, 2003

Website: www.penguin.com

Available in:
Paperback, 336 pages. $14.00
(ISBN 0-14-200174-0)

Subject: Women's Lives/
Americana/Social Issues (Fiction)

Summary

Set in 1964, this story's main character is Lily Owens, whose life has been shaped around the blurred memory of the afternoon her mother was killed. When Lily's fierce-hearted black "stand-in mother," Rosaleen, insults three of the town's fiercest racists, Lily decides they should both escape to Tiburon, South Carolina—a town that holds the secret to her mother's past. There they are taken in by an eccentric trio of black beekeeping sisters who introduce Lily to a mesmerizing world of bees, honey, and the Black Madonna who presides over their household. About divine female power and the transforming power of love, this is a story that women will share and pass on to their daughters for years to come.

Recommended by: Connie May Fowler, author

"A wonderful novel about mothers and daughters and the transcendent power of love."

Author Biography

Sue Monk Kidd is the author of two widely acclaimed nonfiction books, **The Dance of the Dissident Daughter** and **When the Heart Waits**. She has won a Poets and Writers Award for the story that began this novel, as well as a Katherine Anne Porter Award. **The Secret Life of Bees**, her first novel, was nominated for the prestigious Orange Prize in England. Kidd lives beside a salt marsh near Charleston, South Carolina.

Topics to Consider

1) Were you surprised to learn that T. Ray used to be different, that once he truly loved Deborah? How do you think Deborah's leaving affected him? Did it shed any light on why T. Ray was so cruel and abusive to Lily?

2) Had you ever heard of "kneeling on grits?" What qualities did Lily have that allowed her to survive, endure, and eventually thrive, despite T. Ray?

3) Who is the queen bee in this story?

4) Lily's relationship to her dead mother was complex, ranging from guilt to idealization, to hatred, to acceptance. What happens to a daughter when she discovers her mother once abandoned her? Is Lily right—would people generally rather die than forgive? Was it harder for Lily to forgive her mother or herself?

5) Lily grew up without her mother, but in the end she finds a house full of them. Have you ever had a mother figure in your life who wasn't your true mother? Have you ever had to leave home to find home?

6) What compelled Rosaleen to spit on the three men's shoes? What does it take for a person to stand up with conviction against brutalizing injustice? What did you like best about Rosaleen?

7) Had you ever heard of the Black Madonna? What do you think of the story surrounding the Black Madonna in the novel? How would the story be different if it had been a picture of a white Virgin Mary? Do you know women whose lives have been deepened or enriched by a connection to an empowering Divine Mother?

8) Project into the future. Does Lily ever see her father again? Does she become a beekeeper? A writer? What happens to Rosaleen? What happens to Lily and Zach? Who would Zach be today?

For a complete reader's guide, visit www.penguin.com

THE SONG READER

Author: Lisa Tucker

Publisher: Pocket Books (S&S), 2003

Website: www.lisatucker.com

Available in:
Paperback, 306 pages. $12.00
(ISBN 0-7434-6445-1)

Subject: Family Life/
Americana/Identity (Fiction)

Summary

Leeann's older sister Mary Beth has a gift. When the two sisters are left alone after the death of their mother and the disappearance of their father, Mary Beth becomes the hero of both her younger sister and their entire town. She is a "song reader." She doesn't read palms or tarot cards; she reads people's secrets and desires from the songs they can't get out of their minds. And her customers idolize her. But as Leeann soon learns, every gift has its price. The sisters' bond will be tested when Mary Beth's advice leads to a tragedy that divides their small Missouri town. As Mary Beth retreats into her own world, Leeann must face the truth about their parents and their past, and the flawed humanity of the sister she adores.

Recommended by: Silas House, author, *A Parchment of Leaves*

"A stunning debut by a major new voice for her generation."

Author Biography

Lisa Tucker grew up in Missouri, and has toured the Midwest with a jazz band, has worked as a waitress, writing teacher, office cleaner, and math professor. She lives with her husband and son in northern New Mexico, where she has just finished a new novel, ***Shout Down the Moon***.

Topics to Consider

1) Mary Beth was keenly aware of people's thoughts and feelings, yet she wasn't always able to transfer this knowledge to deal with her own situations with her sister, father, Ben, and even herself. Leeann, a teen with a reputation for being lighthearted and carefree, seems better able to address feelings and memories on a personal level. Mary Beth's secrets haunt her, her inability to deal with her own memories tortures her. How does this shape their lives?

2) Tommy, like Leeann and Mary Beth's mother, is an orphan. Why is Mary Beth inclined to take in an abandoned child?

3) Leeann's quest to find her father is an important part of the book. Knowing what she does about how ill her father is, why does she call on him for help? Does Leeann ever really find her father? If so, at what point in the story does she find him? Describe what you feel for Leeann's father.

4) The '80s have been characterized as a time when people began to talk openly about family problems and examine how their past influenced their present. The author artfully takes us back to the decade through pop culture references the records, the record players, letters and the popular songs. How would this novel have worked differently had it been set in today's culture of CDs, MP3s, e-mail, music videos and Oprah?

5) In several instances, walls play an important part in the story—when the sisters discover their dad's lists written on walls, when Mary Beth recreates her surroundings in the apartment after Leeann's accident and when Juanita reveals Mary Beth's first painting project in the basement of the old family home. What message is the author writing on the walls?

As a special promotion, Lisa Tucker will talk by phone to any book club that chooses **The Song Reader.** *To schedule a time and date, visit her website, www.lisatucker.com.*

A THREAD OF GRACE

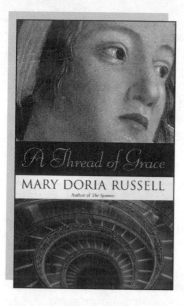

Author: Mary Doria Russell

Publisher: Random House (Feb. '05)

Website: www.athreadofgrace.com

Available in:
Hardcover, 464 pages. $25.95
(ISBN 0-375-50184-3)

Subject: Jewish Studies/
Cultural & World Issues
(Historical Fiction)

Summary

It is September 8, 1943, and fourteen-year-old Claudette Blum is learning Italian with a suitcase in her hand. She and her father are among the thousands of Jewish refugees scrambling over the Alps toward Italy, where they hope to be safe at last, now that the Italians have broken with Germany and made a separate peace with the Allies. The Blums soon discover that Italy is anything but peaceful, as it becomes, overnight, an open battleground pitting against one another the Nazis, the Allies, resistance fighters, Jews in hiding, and ordinary Italians trying to survive. Through a handful of fascinating characters, **Mary Doria Russell** tells the little known but true story of the network of Italian citizens who saved the lives of forty-three thousand Jews during the final twenty months of the war.

Author Biography

The author of prize-winning research in paleoanthropology, **Mary Doria Russell** has written two previous novels, *The Sparrow* and *Children of God*, which have won several international literary awards and remain favorites of reading groups around the country. She lives with her husband and son in Cleveland, Ohio.

Mary Doria Russell will be available for book group phone chats. For more information, see page 73.

Topics to Consider

1) Renzo and Schramm have both committed crimes against civilians during war, but the priest Don Osvaldo feels there is some essential difference between the two men's actions. Is the difference merely a matter of scale, or is there an ethical difference? How does your emotional response to each character color your opinion?

2) Renzo attempts to remain apolitical during the Nazi occupation. Was that a moral position or should he have fought the Nazis from the beginning? Is moderation or neutrality possible or even desirable during war?

3) We are accustomed to admiring the partisan resistance to German occupation during World War II. In today's world there are many places where armed resistance to occupying forces is called "terrorism." What makes a resistance legitimate? Does the motive of the occupying force make any difference?

4) Claudette's children never understand her, and she dies a mystery to them. Have you been affected by the war experiences of a family member? Were you aware of how their experiences deformed them?

5) Was Iacopo Soncini a bad husband or a good rabbi? How does having a family change the responsibilities of the clergy?

6) Imagine that you heard Schramm's confession at the beginning of the book. If you were Don Osvaldo, what would you have told Schramm? Are there unforgivable sins?

7) Was Schramm's remorse genuine at the end of the book? Why did he put his uniform back on when he was ordered to by the German officer at the hospital?

8) How would you feel about a moral universe where Schramm went to heaven and Renzo went to hell?

9) People who didn't live through World War II often believe they would have hidden someone like Anne Frank or helped refugees from Nazi Germany the way the Italian peasants did. What would be an analogous risk today?

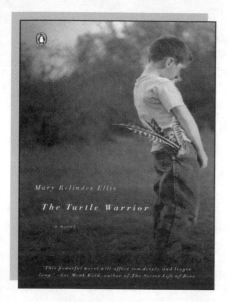

THE TURTLE WARRIOR

Author: Mary Relindes Ellis

Publisher: Penguin (Feb. '05)

Website: www.penguin.com

Available in:
Paperback, 384 pages. $14.00
(ISBN 0-14-303452-9)

Subject: Family Life/Americana/
Personal Triumph (Fiction)

Summary

The Lucases live in the beautiful, isolated country of Northern Wisconsin, inhabited by working class European immigrants and the Ojibwe. By 1967, their farm has fallen into disrepair, thanks to the hard drinking of John Lucas, who brutalizes his wife and sons. When the eldest, James, escapes by enlisting to fight in Vietnam, he leaves young Bill behind to protect his mother Claire, who struggles to maintain a hold on reality. Bill, after his father's sudden death, begins to drink himself into oblivion. Their neighbors, Ernie and Rosemary, offer the Lucas family their only contact with a normal life and the warmth and love that might save them. In much the same vein as Louise Erdrich and Wally Lamb, **Mary Ellis** dramatizes the many ways that violence and abuse cycle through families and threaten to utterly extinguish the human spirit. But what she affirms most convincingly is love's power to transcend and transform that suffering into joy.

Recommended by: Sue Monk Kidd, author

"...This powerful novel will affect you deeply and linger long."

Author Biography

Mary Relindes Ellis was born and raised in northern Wisconsin. Her stories have appeared in *The Milwaukee Journal*, the anthology *Uncommon Waters: Women Write About Fishing*, and *Glimmer Train* magazine. **The Turtle Warrior** is her first novel.

Topics to Consider

1) In what ways is the snapping turtle, both literally and symbolically, important to the novel? Why would Bill call himself the "Turtle Warrior?" In what ways does he come out of his shell by the end of the book?

2) At what crucial moments in the novel does the failure to speak, to communicate one's deepest or most painful feelings, cause harm? Why would Ernie, particularly, feel such grief over words unspoken?

3) Mary Relindes Ellis employs an unusual narrative strategy in *The Turtle Warrior*, retelling the same events from different points of view. How does this way of telling the story affect how we read the novel?

4) Why would the inability to cry make one dangerous? In what ways does the open expression of pain and grief save Billy and Ernie at the end of the novel?

5) How would you explain the extreme violence—from John Lucas's abuse of his wife and sons to the war in Vietnam—that occurs in *The Turtle Warrior*? What are the connections between violence in families and violence between nations?

6) In what ways is Claire's predicament typical of women trapped in abusive relationships? What options does Claire have? Should she have left her husband? Why doesn't she?

7) In what ways does Jimmy's spirit "cling" to his family? At what crucial moments does he appear or communicate with the living? What effect do these communications have?

8) In what ways does reading *The Turtle Warrior* itself offer both an escape from, and a deeper connection with, one's own life? In what ways is it diverting? In what ways does it explore the basic human dilemmas we all experience in one form or another?

For a complete reader's guide, visit www.penguin.com

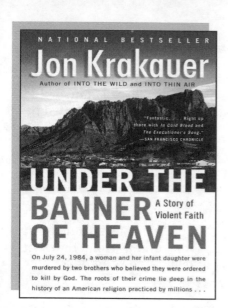

UNDER THE BANNER OF HEAVEN

Author: Jon Krakauer

Publisher: Anchor Books, 2004

Website:
www.readinggroupcenter.com

Available in:
Paperback, 423 pages. $14.95
(ISBN 1-4000-3280-6)

Subject: Social Issues/Faith
(Nonfiction)

Summary

In *Under the Banner of Heaven*, Jon Krakauer shifts his focus from extremes of physical adventure (*Into Thin Air*) to extremes of religious belief within our own borders. At the core of his book is an appalling double murder committed by two Mormon Fundamentalist brothers, Ron and Dan Lafferty, who insist they received a revelation from God commanding them to kill their blameless victims. Beginning with a meticulously researched account of this "divinely inspired" crime, Krakauer constructs a multilayered, bone-chilling narrative of messianic delusion, savage violence, polygamy, and unyielding faith. Along the way, he uncovers a shadowy offshoot of America's fastest-growing religion, and raises provocative questions about the nature of religious belief.

Recommended by: *San Francisco Chronicle*

"Fantastic.... Right up there with In Cold Blood *and* The Executioner's Song.*"*

Author Biography

Jon Krakauer is the author of *Eiger Dreams, Into the Wild*, and *Into Thin Air*, and is editor of the Modern Library Exploration series.

Topics to Consider

1) What does the book reveal about fanatics such as Ron and Dan Lafferty? What does it reveal about brutality and faith and the connections between them?

2) Why does Krakauer move back and forth between Mormon history and contemporary events? What are the connections between the beliefs and practices of Joseph Smith and his followers in the nineteenth century and the behavior of people like Dan and Ron Lafferty, Brian David Mitchell, and others in the twentieth?

3) How does polygamy affect young girls? Is it, as prosecutor David Leavitt claims, pedophilia plain and simple?

4) When Krakauer asks Dan Lafferty if he has considered the parallels between himself and Osama bin Laden, Dan asserts that bin Laden is a "child of the Devil" and that the hijackers were "following a false prophet," whereas he is following a true prophet. No doubt, bin Laden would say much the same of Lafferty. How are Dan Lafferty and Osama bin Laden alike? In what ways are all religious fundamentalists alike?

5) Given the nature of, and motive for, the murders of Brenda Lafferty and her child, should Ron Lafferty be considered mentally ill? If so, should all others who "talk to God" or receive revelations—a central tenant of Mormonism—also be considered mentally ill? What would the legal ramifications be of such a shift in thought?

6) At the very end of the book, former Mormon fundamentalist DeLoy Bateman says that while the Mormon fundamentalists who live within Colorado City may be happier than those who live outside it, he believes that "some things in life are more important than being happy. Like being free to think for yourself" [p. 334]. Why does Krakauer end the book this way? Are there ways in which Mormons are not free to think for themselves? If so, would they apply to other religions as well? Is such freedom more important than happiness?

For a complete Reading Group Guide, visit
www.readinggroupcenter.com

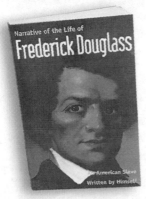

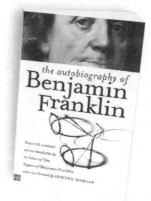

AUTHOR PHONE CHATS
FROM THE RANDOM HOUSE PUBLISHING GROUP

The only thing more satisfying than reading a good book is the discussion that follows. Every month, we offer book clubs a chance to **WIN A PHONE CHAT WITH A SELECTED AUTHOR.** All you need is a speakerphone . . . we'll take care of the rest!

Sarah Dunant, author of *The Birth of Venus*
(Random House trade paperback, on sale November 30, 0-8129-6897-2)

Mary Doria Russell, author of *A Thread of Grace*
(Random House hardcover, on sale February 1, 0-375-50184-3)

Elizabeth Berg, author of *The Art of Mending*
(Ballantine Reader's Circle trade paperback, on sale March 1, 0-8129-7098-5)

Sonny Brewer, author of *The Poet of Tolstoy Park*
(Ballantine hardcover, on sale March 1, 0-345-47631-X)

Diane Hammond, author of *Going to Bend*
(Ballantine Reader's Circle trade paperback, on sale March 1, 0-345-46098-7)

Samantha Gillison, author of *The King of America*
(Random House trade paperback, on sale April 12, 0-375-76075-X)

For more details visit us at www.authorphonechat.com

The Random House Publishing Group

Bookstore Tourism

The Book Addict's Guide to
Planning & Promoting
Bookstore Road Trips
for Bibliophiles & Other Bookshop Junkies

LARRY PORTZLINE

An innovative grassroots effort
to promote and support independent bookstores
by marketing them as a tourist destination
and creating a new travel niche for booklovers

Bookshop Junkie Press
www.bookstoretourism.com
ISBN 0-9758934-0-8
Distributed by Ingram and Baker & Taylor

RESOURCES

The Internet

Reading Group Choices Online — guides available from major publishers and independent presses that can be printed directly from the site: **www.readinggroupchoices.com**

For new book information, reading lists, book news and literary events, visit **ReadingGroupGuides.com, generousbooks.com, BookSpot.com**, and **BookMuse.com**. Looking for reading guides for children? Visit **KidsReads.com**.

Publisher Web Sites — Find additional topics for discussion, special offers for book groups, and other titles of interest.

Algonquin Books of Chapel Hill — *algonquin.com*
Anchor Books — *readinggroupcenter.com*
Ballantine Books — *ballantinereaderscircle.com*
Doubleday Books — *doubleday.com*
Grove/Atlantic — *groveatlantic.com*
HarperCollins — *harpercollins.com*
Hyperion Books — *hyperionbooks.com*
In One Press — *inonepress.com*
Knopf Books — *aaknopf.com*
Little, Brown & Co. — *twbookmark.com*
Middleway Press — *middlewaypress.org*
W.W. Norton — *wwnorton.com*
Penguin/Putnam — *penguin.com*
Picador — *picadorusa.com*
Platinum One — *platinumonepublishing.com*
Plume Books — *penguin.com*
Pocket Books — *simonsays.com*
Random House — *randomhouse.com*
Red Wheel/Weiser/Conari — *redwheelweiser.com*
Simon & Schuster — *simonsays.com*
Tor Books — *tor.com*
Vintage Books — *readinggroupcenter.com*
Warner Books — *twbookmark.com*
Yale University Press — *yalebooks.com*

Newsletters and Book Lists

BookWomen: A Readers' Community for Those Who Love Women's Words, a bimonthly "bookletter" published by the Minnesota Women's Press. Includes recommendations, news about the book world, and articles for and about women readers and writers.
Subscription: $24/yr. (6 issues). Contact: **books@womenspress.com**
Minnesota Women's Press
771 Raymond Ave.
St. Paul, MN 55114
(651) 646-3968

Reverberations News Journal, Rachel Jacobsohn's publication of the Association of Book Group Readers and Leaders.
Annual membership including subscription is $20.
Contact: **rachelj@attbi.com**

Books & Journals

Bibliotherapy: The Girl's Guide to Books for Every Phase of Our Lives by Nancy Peske and Beverly West.
Published by DTP, ISBN 0-4405-0897-5, $14.95.

The Book Club Cookbook: Recipes and Food for Thought from Your Book Club's Favorite Books and Authors by Judy Gelman and Vicki Levy Krupp.
Published by Tarcher/Penguin, ISBN 1-58542-322-X, $15.95.

The Book Group Book: A Thoughtful Guide to Forming and Enjoying a Stimulating Book Discussion Group.
Edited by Ellen Slezak and Margaret Eleanor Atwood.
Published by Chicago Review Press, ISBN 1-5565-2412-9, $14.95.

Circles of Sisterhood: A Book Discussion Group Guide for Women of Color by Pat Neblett.
Published by Writers & Readers, ISBN 0-8631-6245-2, $14.

Contemporary Multi-Ethnic Novels by Women Coming of Age Together in the New America by Rochelle Holt, Ph.D.
Published by Thanks Be to Grandmother Winifred Foundation, $5 + SASE (6" by 8"). Write to:
15223 Coral Isle Ct., Ft. Myers, FL 33919.

Family Book Sharing Groups: Start One in Your Neighborhood!
By Marjorie R. Simic with Eleanor C. MacFarlane.
Published by the Family Literacy Center, 1-8837-9011-5, $6.95.

*Literature Circles: Voice and Choice in Book Clubs
and Reading Groups* by Harvey Daniels.
Published by Stenhouse Publishers, ISBN 1-5711-0333-3, $22.50.

Minnesota Women's Press Great Books. An annotated listing of 236
books by women authors chosen by over 3,000 women participating
in Minnesota Women's Press Book Groups in the past 13 years.
$10.95 + $2 s/h. (612) 646-3968.

*The Mother-Daughter Book Club: How Ten Busy Mothers and
Daughters Came Together to Talk, Laugh and Learn Through
Their Love of Reading* by Shireen Dodson and Teresa Barker.
Published by HarperCollins, ISBN 0-0609-5242-3, $14.

The Readers' Choice: 200 Book Club Favorites by Victoria McMains.
Published by Wm. Morrow, ISBN 0-6881-7435-3, $14.

*The Reading Group Handbook: Everything You Need to Know to
Start Your Own Book Club* by Rachel Jacobsohn.
Published by Hyperion, ISBN 0-786-88324-3, $12.95.

*The Reading List: Contemporary Fiction, A Critical Guide to the
Complete Works of 125 Authors*. Edited by David Rubel.
Published by Owl Books, ISBN 0-805055-27-4, $17.

Reading to Heal: A Reading Group Strategy for Better Health
by Diane Dawber.
Published by Quarry Press, ISBN 1-5508-2229-2, $9.95.

*Talking About Books: Literature Discussion Groups in
K-8 Classrooms* by Kathy Short.
Published by Heinemann, ISBN 0-3250-0073-5, $24.

*What to Read: The Essential Guide for Reading Group Members
and Other Book Lovers (Revised)* by Mickey Pearlman.
Published by HarperCollins, ISBN 0-0609-5313-6, $14.

*A Year of Reading: A Month-By-Month Guide to Classics
and Crowd-Pleasers for You or Your Book Group*
by H. E. Ellington and Jane Freimiller.
Published by Sourcebooks, ISBN 1-5707-1935-7, $14.95.

BOOK GROUP MEMBERS

Name _____

    Day phone _____ Eve. phone _____

Name _____

    Day phone _____ Eve. phone_____

Name _____

    Day phone _____ Eve. phone_____

Name _____

    Day phone _____ Eve. phone_____

Name _____

    Day phone _____ Eve. phone_____

Name _____

    Day phone _____ Eve. phone_____

Name _____

    Day phone _____ Eve. phone_____

Name _____

    Day phone _____ Eve. phone_____

Name _____

    Day phone _____ Eve. phone_____

Name _____

    Day phone _____ Eve. phone_____

Name _____

    Day phone _____ Eve. phone_____

INDEX BY SUBJECT/INTEREST AREA

WHAT OTHER GROUPS HAVE READ —
AND ENJOYED

Early in 2004, we asked book groups on **Reading Group Choices Online** to tell us about the books they read and discussed during the previous year that they enjoyed most. It's always interesting to see the hundreds of titles that get recommended—and which ones appear in the top 20.

What were your favorites of 2004?

Visit us online and with your entry, you'll have the chance to receive books for each person in your group (compliments of one of our publishing partners) and a check for $75 to cater one of your next meetings.

**Register January 1 — March 31, 2005
At www.readinggroupchoices.com**

BOOK GROUP FAVORITES FROM 2003

1. *The Secret Life of Bees* by Sue Monk Kidd (Viking)

2. *The Da Vinci Code* by Dan Brown (Doubleday)

3. *The Red Tent* by Anita Diamant (Picador USA)

4. *Seabiscuit* by Laura Hillenbrand (Random House)

5. *Life of Pi* by Yann Martel (Harcourt)

6. *Girl With a Pearl Earring* by Tracy Chevalier (Plume)

7. *Peace Like a River* by Leif Enger (Grove)

8. *Bel Canto* by Ann Patchett (HarperCollins)

9. *The Lovely Bones* by Alice Sebold (Little Brown)

10. *Empire Falls* by Richard Russo (Knopf)

11. *Middlesex* by Jeffrey Eugenides (Picador USA)

12. *#1 Ladies Detective Agency* by Alexander McCall Smith (Anchor)

13. *Pope Joan* by Donna Woolfolk Cross (Ballantine)

14. *Atonement* by Ian McEwan (Anchor)

15. *Cold Mountain* by Charles Frasier (Vintage)